A Revelation Bombshell

A Revelation Bombshell

A Deeper Analysis of Revelation 3:10

Charles Cooper

The Truth About Revelation 3:10

R eady to be shocked? Mind-boggled? Stupefied? Here's a little-known fact. You may want to believe it. You might not. You might resist believing it because, after all, most people you know probably do. How could so many good men and women be wrong? But it's still true nonetheless. Ready?

Revelation 3:10 does not prove a pretribulation rapture of the church.

For pretribulationists, Revelation 3:10 is the single most important verse on the timing of the rapture. At first glance, the verse looks like a very simple promise:

"Because thou hast kept the word of my patience, I also will keep thee from the hour of temptation, which shall come upon all the world, to try them that dwell upon the earth." (KJV)

1

A Revelation Bombshell

Here are some quotes on the importance of this verse from some of the world's most renowned prophecy teachers and seminary professors whose books line the shelves of many Christian bookstores and libraries:

1. "It's the best exegetical proof of a pretribulational rapture of the Church."

2. "It's the determining passage."

3. "The Philadelphian church is promised escape from the tribulation."

4. "If there is a 'proof text' for the pretribulational position, it is Revelation 3:10."

5. "Revelation 3:10 has remained the primary defense of the pretribulational position."

6. "Here, then, is a promise which clearly indicates the pretribulational rapture of the Church."

7. "This promise, however, is to the church of Philadelphia: she will be raptured before the Tribulation begins. It seems difficult to understand why some false teachers suggest that the Church must go through the Tribulation in view of this clear-cut statement of our Lord."

8. "One of the best promises guaranteeing the Church's rapture before the Tribulation is

found in Revelation 3:10."

9. "It's the only passage in Revelation to speak of the rapture."

10. "This verse promises that the Church will be delivered from the Tribulation."

11. "It's the primary understanding of the pretribulational rapture of the Church."

12. "We clearly see in this promise that the Church will not go through the Tribulation."

13. "There are certain passages of Scripture which definitely promise the church's removal before the 70th Week."

Who are the men who have said these things? What if it can be proven beyond a shadow of a doubt that every one of these men was sincere, albeit sincerely *wrong*? What if there is not one passage in the New Testament that explicitly supports a pretribulational rapture, including Revelation 3:10? Confronted with this truth, what would you do?

This truth starts with the fact that there is an error in the translation of this often-cited verse. Technically, the error is not with the translation. All of the English words necessary to communicate the intended meaning of the Greek language (which John used to communicate God's message to us) are present. The error is found in one little period, which you will discover later.

A Revelation Bombshell

The Power of Commas and Periods

English speakers know the power of commas and periods.

Examples:

1. Let's eat, Tweety!
2. Let's eat Tweety!

1. Woman, without her man, is nothing.
2. Woman, without her, man is nothing.

1. Jim needs a camera, battery, and case.
2. Jim needs a camera battery and case.

Whether Tweety eats with us or is eaten by us is important to Tweety. Whether a man honors his woman or his woman honors him all depends on comma placement. Whether a child's father spends $1,000 or $100 also depends on the placement of the comma.

Perhaps one of the most interesting examples of the power of commas comes from the book by Lynne Truss: *Eats, Shoots, and Leaves*:

A panda walks into a cafe. He orders a sandwich, eats it, then draws a gun and fires two shots in the air. "Why?" asks the confused waiter, as the panda makes towards the exit. The panda produces a badly punctuated wildlife manual and tosses it over his shoulder. "I'm a panda," he says at the door. "Look it up." The waiter turns to the relevant entry, and sure enough, finds an explanation. "Panda. Large black-and-white bear-like mammal, native to China. Eats, shoots and leaves."

The correct placement of a period is equally important in Scripture.

Divisions of Man

The original Hebrew and Greek manuscripts did not have punctuation or chapter and verse divisions. This fact has a profound impact on our interpretation of Revelation 3:10. Let's start with some history.

In the mid-1200s, one man, Cardinal Hugo de Sancto Caro, started the chapter and verse divisions we have become so familiar with. But the person typically credited with the modern chapter divisions is Stephen Langton, an Archbishop of Canterbury in England, who began the process around 1227 A.D. The original Wycliffe English Bible utilized his system in 1382.

As for the verses, the system we see today was put into place by Robert Estienne, who used the numbered verse system when printing the Bible in 1551 or 1555. Since the time of the Geneva Bible Version (an English version published in Paris, 1560), which preceded the King James

A Revelation Bombshell

Version, nearly all Bible versions have used this same numbering system.

Nothing about the chapter and verse divisions is inspired. It is a widely accepted technique created by man to help the reader easily find certain passages of Scripture. How the text is punctuated is also an agreed-upon device of man. Neither the Hebrew nor the Greek utilized punctuation similar to our modern system.

How, then, were the translators able to decide where to end one verse and begin another? Both the Greek and Hebrew have certain words that indicate a transition in thought. Just as in English, certain words indicate a change in the flow of the thought patterns of the writer. For example, *therefore* indicates that the writer is drawing a conclusion about something previously stated. There are many such words in Koine Greek, which is the language used to record God's Word in the original New Testament manuscripts.

The great majority of chapter and verse divisions in the Bible are correct. Either on the basis of grammar, thought unit, logic, or some other indicator, the translators got it right. However, there are several critical places where they did not. Revelation 3:10 is one of them.

Before we define the error and its solution, let's look at the consequences of a faulty translation.

The Timing of the Rapture:
The Importance of Revelation 3:10 to the Debate

In 1973, Dr. Robert H. Gundry published a groundbreaking response to the pretribulation rapture position entitled *The Church and the Tribulation*. In his book, he declared Revelation 3:10 to be "probably the most debated verse in the whole discussion about the time of the Church's rapture."[1] Gundry's assessment is no doubt true because his statement is regularly quoted in every subsequently published book or article that offers insight into the interpretation of this verse.

Why can't scholars come to an agreement concerning the simple meaning of this passage? If you keep reading, you will see that the reason is because they have been trying to squeeze a square peg into a round hole.

---

[1] Robert H. Gundry, *The Church and the Tribulation* (Grand Rapids: Zondervan Publishing House, 1973), 54.

A Revelation Bombshell

Notice the importance of Revelation 3:10 to those who defend a pretribulational rapture. Michael J. Svigel, assistant professor of theological studies at Dallas Theological Seminary, wrote an article that appeared in *Trinity Journal* (Spring 2001) entitled "The Apocalypse of John and the Rapture of the Church: a Re-evaluation." In this article, Svigel discusses the various views regarding where in the sequence of the book one should place the rapture of the church. Before presenting his personal view, Svigel canvasses the various positions put forth by scholarly proponents. The very first position he highlights is the classic pretribulation position.

Regarding Revelation 3:10, he states,

The promise of protection in Rev 3:10 is considered by many commentators to be *the best exegetical proof* of a pretribulational Rapture of the Church.[2] (italic added)

The best exegetical proof of a pretribulational rapture of the church. Those are extremely significant words. To date, no pretribulationist has disagreed with Svigel's assessment. Thus, we can take this conclusion to be an accurate portrayal of those listed in this booklet who also support the pretrib view.

What does "exegetical proof" mean? In case you are not familiar with the term, let me explain. *Exegetical* is an adjective that comes from the noun *exegesis*, which is a transliteration of an ancient Greek verb that means literally "to lead out." That is, to lead out the meaning of the text. It is typically translated in the Bible as "to explain" or "to interpret." Exegesis "is the application of the rules of interpretation to the passages of Scripture to determine their exact meaning.[3] Thus, an exegetical proof is a meaning derived directly from a passage of Scripture.

Svigel contends that many commentators believe that the doctrine of a pretribulation rapture is derived directly from Revelation 3:10. His statement about *proving* a pretrib rapture leaves little room for debate. Obviously,

---

[2] Michael J. Svigel, "The Apocalypse of John and the Rapture of the Church: a Reevaluation," *TJ 22* (Spring 2001), 25.

[3] *Vol. 137: Bibliotheca Sacra Volume 137.* 1980 (546) (152). Dallas, TX: Dallas Theological Seminary.

A Revelation Bombshell

we need to know who these people are and what they have said specifically. Svigel offers a list of Bible teachers who would agree with his statement that Revelation 3:10 *proves* a pretribulation rapture. It is a list of the veritable "who's who" in conservative scholarship.

The Best Exegetical Proof

Dr. Lewis Sperry Chafer

First on the list is Dr. Lewis Sperry Chafer, the founder and first president of Dallas Theological Seminary. He wrote an eight-volume set of books on systematic theology first published in 1947.

Chafer writes that when considering the biblical basis of a pretribulation rapture, "The *determining passage* is Revelation 3:10"[4] (italics added). In Dr. Chafer's opinion, Revelation 3:10 is "the determining passage" in support of a pretribulational rapture as defined by classical pretribulationists. This means that *there is no other passage in the Bible* that proves a pretrib rapture the way Revelation 3:10 does. Of course, we know that a sword cuts both ways. In this case, if Revelation 3:10 is the

_____

[4] Lewis Sperry Chafer, *Ecclesiology, Eschatology*, Vol. 4 (Dallas: Dallas Seminary, 1948), 369–71.

determining passage, then without it, there is no passage that "determines" a pretrib rapture. In essence, outside of Revelation 3:10, there is no other passage in the Bible that proves it.

Since no subsequent president of Dallas Theological Seminary or any of the hundreds of very able professors who have taught or who are now teaching there have corrected or disputed Dr. Chafer's claim, we conclude that this remains the official position of Dallas Theological Seminary.

The Determining Passage

Dr. Paul D. Feinberg

Svigel lists Dr. Paul D. Feinberg as a second proponent who would say that Revelation 3:10 is the best exegetical proof of a pretribulational rapture. Among his many teaching posts, Feinberg was a professor of biblical and systematic theology at Trinity Evangelical Divinity School. In his article "The Case for the Pretribulation Rapture Position" published in *Three Views on the Rapture: Pre-, Mid-, or Post-Tribulational?* in 1984, Feinberg states, "The texts that express this promise are: 1 Thessalonians 1:10; 5:9;

A Revelation Bombshell

Revelation 3:10."[5] In plain English, according to Dr. Feinberg, Revelation 3:10 expresses the promise of a pretribulation rapture.

Dr. Henry C. Thiessen

Another listee is Dr. Henry C. Thiessen. In his book, *Lectures in Systematic Theology*, originally published in 1949, he writes, "The promise in Rev. 3:10 points to a pretribulational rapture."[6] In an earlier work, Thiessen also wrote, "We may say that the Philadelphian church is promised escape from the Tribulation."[7]

Dr. David G. Winfrey

Another name on the list is Dr. David G. Winfrey. In the article "The Great Tribulation: Kept 'Out Of' or 'Through'?" written in 1982, he insists, "If there is a 'proof text' for the pretribulational position, it is Rev 3:10."[8]

---

[5] Paul D. Feinberg, "The Case for the Pretribulation Rapture Position," *Three Views on the Rapture: Pre-, Mid-, or Post-Tribulational?* Gleason L. Archer Jr., et al. (Grand Rapids: Zondervan, 1996), 52.

[6] Henry C. Thiessen, *Lectures in Systematic Theology* (Grand Rapids: Eerdmans, 1949), 377.

[7] Henry C. Thiessen, *Will the Church Pass Through the Tribulation?* (New York: Loizeaux Brothers, 1941), 21.

[8] David G. Winfrey, "The Great Tribulation: Kept "Out Of" Or "Through"?" *GTJ* 3 (Spring 1982), 5.

What is a proof text? It is a scriptural passage given as proof for a doctrine or principle. So notice in Winfrey's own words, "If there is a 'proof text' for the pretribulational position, it is Rev 3:10." If that be so, then the converse must also be true—that is, if Revelation 3:10 is not a proof text, then the pretribulational rapture position does not have a proof text.

Additionally, Winfrey adds,

Although several of the texts used to support the pretribulational view have been abandoned by pretribulationists, Rev 3:10 has remained the primary defense of the position.[9]

Primary defense is remarkably strong language. There is no equivocation here. His statement is either true or false, and there is very little room for error in understanding his intent. If Revelation 3:10 is "the primary defense," this means that apart from Revelation 3:10, there is no other passage of Scripture that a person can use as a primary defense of a pretribulational rapture.

---

[9] Ibid., 4.

A Revelation Bombshell

The Primary Defense

Zane C. Hodges

We can also add Zane C. Hodges, former professor at Dallas Theological Seminary, to the list. He states,

> Even proponents of the Pre-tribulation Rapture often defend it as if it results from a series of inferences drawn from scattered biblical texts. Or, they may cite a few isolated proof-texts (like Revelation 3:10).[10]

Hodges echoes Winfrey in believing that Revelation 3:10 is a proof text.

If language means anything, if people are to be taken at their word, if facts are facts, then these men believe that Revelation 3:10 proves beyond a shadow of a doubt that the Bible explicitly teaches a pretribulational rapture.

Dr. Gerald B. Stanton

The noted late professor and Bible teacher Dr. Gerald B. Stanton takes a similar position. In his book

---

[10] Zane C. Hodges, "1 Thessalonians 5:1-11 and the Rapture," *CTSJ* (October 2000), 20.

Kept From the Hour, after quoting Revelation 3:10, he categorically states, "Here, then, is a promise which clearly indicates the pretribulation rapture of the Church."

Dr. Tim LaHaye

World-renowned author and Bible teacher Dr. Tim LaHaye, in a commentary on the book of Revelation, said regarding this verse:

> This promise, however, is to the church of Philadelphia: she will be raptured before that Tribulation begins. It seems difficult to understand why some false teachers suggest that the Church must go through the Tribulation in view of *this clear-cut statement* of our Lord.[11] (italics added)

Again, with the help of Jerry B. Jenkins, LaHaye writes, "One of the best promises guaranteeing the Church's rapture before the Tribulation is found in Revelation 3:10."[12]

---

[11] Tim LaHaye, *Revelation Unveiled* (Grand Rapids: Zondervan Publishing House, 1999), 81.

[12] Tim LaHaye and Jerry B. Jenkins, *Are We Living in the End Times?* (Wheaton: Tyndale House Publishers, 1999), 107.

A Revelation Bombshell

Dr. Keith H. Essex

Keith H. Essex, assistant professor of Bible exposition at The Master's Seminary, wrote an article in 2002 entitled "The Rapture and the Book of Revelation." In it, he argues that there are ten passages in the book of Revelation which are proposed references to the rapture. He concludes, "An evaluation of these then leads to Rev 3:10-11 as *the only passage* in Revelation to speak of the rapture."[13]

Dr. Jeffery L. Townsend

Regarding Revelation 3:10, Dr. Jeffery L. Townsend, one-time pastor at Believers Bible Church in Texas, wrote,

> Equally sincere and devout students of the prophetic Scriptures hold differing views on the time of the rapture of the church in relation to the tribulation. This is due in large measure to the fact that no verse of Scripture specifically states that relationship. But Revelation 3:10 *comes close.*[14] (italics added)

---

[13] Keith H. Essex, "The Rapture and the Book of Revelation," *MSJ* 13 (Fall 2002), 214.
[14] Jeffrey L. Townsend, "The Rapture in Revelation 3:10," *BSac* 137 (July 1980), 248.

16

Dr. John MacArthur, Jr.

John MacArthur, Jr., president of The Master's College and Seminary and senior pastor of Grace Community Church in California, commenting on Revelation 3:10, states, "This verse promises that the church will be delivered from the Tribulation, thus supporting a pretribulation Rapture."[15]

Dr. David Hocking

David Hocking, a Christian Bible teacher heard on the radio around the world, in a paper presented at the 2007 Pre-Trib Study Group Conference entitled "The Rapture in Revelation," states, "It is this one verse that gives the primary understanding of the pretribulational rapture of the Church."[16]

Dr. David Jeremiah

David Jeremiah, senior pastor of Shadow Mountain Community Church (El Cajon, California), makes comments regarding this critical verse, as well. These

---

[15] John MacArthur, Jr., Revelation 1-11, MNTC (Chicago: Moody Press, 1991), 124.
[16] http://www.pre-trib.org/data/pdf/Hocking-TheRaptureinRevelati.pdf (p. 3).

A Revelation Bombshell

comments are typical of the dogmatic conclusions many claim regarding Revelation 3:10. He writes,

> This refers to the rapture, when Jesus will catch away God's people for Himself. We are pre-Tribulational in our beliefs, and we clearly see in this promise that the church will not go through the Tribulation. How can the clarity of this promise be explained any other way?[17]

Dr. Richard Mayhue

Dr. Richard Mayhue, executive vice president and dean of The Master's Seminary, states, "Rev. 3:10 promises that the church will be removed prior to Daniel's Seventieth Week."[18]

Dr. Allen Beechick

Dr. Allen Beechick, graduate of Western Conservative Baptist Seminary in Portland, Oregon and author of several books on the pretribulation rapture,

---

[17] David Jeremiah, *Escape the Coming Night* (Nashville: Thomas Nelson, 1990), 55.
[18] Richard Mayhue, "Why a Pretribulational Rapture?" *TMSJ* (Fall 2002), 247.

states, "Revelation 3:10 gives a wonderful promise to the church that she will not go through the tribulation."[19]

Regarding this verse, Beechick also lists seven reasons the rapture cannot come after the tribulation. Reason number five is as follows: "Revelation 3:10 clearly says, 'I will keep you from the hour.' . . . What could be clearer than that?"[20]

Dr. J. Dwight Pentecost

In connection with the importance of Revelation 3:10 to the rapture debate, J. Dwight Pentecost, distinguished professor emeritus of Bible exposition and adjunct professor in Bible exposition at Dallas Theological Seminary, as well as author of *Things to Come*, writes, "There are certain passages of Scripture which definitely promise the church a removal before the seventieth week."[21]

---

[19] Allen Beechick, *The Pretribulation Rapture* (Denver: Accent Books, 1980), 164.

[20] http://www.rapturesolution.com/beechick/Intro/7reasons.htm (last accessed April 25, 2012)

[2121] J. Dwight Pentecost, *Things to Come* (Findley, Ohio: Dunham Publishing Company, 1963), 216.

A Revelation Bombshell

Dr. Robert L. Thomas

With Robert L. Thomas, professor of New Testament at The Master's Seminary and executive editor of *The Master's Seminary Journal*, we notice a less dogmatic stance about the significance of Revelation 3:10. He states,

> Pretribulationists have often cited Revelation 3:10 as one of the strongest evidences for Christ's coming to remove the church before Daniel's seventieth week, and rightly so. . . . Yet the verse does not explicitly speak of the rapture so much as it tells of the church's preservation at a location away from the scene of earthly tribulation during that period.[22]

James A. Borland

James A. Borland, professor of theology and Bible at Liberty Baptist Seminary, states, "A . . . key pretribulation rapture verse is Revelation 3:10."[23]

---

[22] Robert L. Thomas, "The 'Comings' of Christ in Revelation 2-3," *MSJ* 7 (Fall 1996), 172.

[23] James A. Borland, "Reassessing and Reconfirming the Major Arguments for a Pretribulational Rapture," a paper presented at the Eastern Regional [meeting of the Evangelical Theological Society], Myerstown, PA, March 6, 1999.

Thomas D. Ice

Thomas D. Ice, executive director of the Pre-Trib Research Center, states, "Revelation 3:10 is known as a verse that supports the pretribulational rapture."[24]

Dr. John F. Walvoord

Dr. John F. Walvoord, the second president of Dallas Theological Seminary and perhaps the best known modern defender of the pretribulation rapture, writes, "This statement [Revelation 3:10-11] implies a pretribulation rapture."[25]

Michael J. Svigel

After arguing both for and against the notion that Revelation 3:10 is a rapture passage in his article, Michael J. Svigel himself concludes,

These debatable variables effectively relegate Rev 3:10 to *a position of secondary significance* or corroborative evidence with regard to the Rapture

---

[24] Thomas D. Ice, "The Meaning of 'Earth Dwellers' in Revelation," *BSac* 166 (July-September 2009), 350.
[25] John F. Walvoord, *Prophecy in the New Millennium* (Grand Rapids: Kregel Publications, 2001), 34.

A Revelation Bombshell

of the Church in the Apocalypse of John.[26] (italics added)

In less than sixty years, we have gone from the dogmatic assertion of Dr. Lewis Sperry Chafer that Revelation 3:10 is *the determining passage* to Michael J. Svigel, while a graduate student at Dallas Theological Seminary, who relegates it to *a position of secondary significance*. But it gets worse. Dr. John Niemelä, a prominent fellow pretribber, is forced to conclude that the verse has nothing to do with the definition of the traditional pretrib rapture position at all. What are the consequences of this change? This question will be answered in the next section.

Before we do that, let's reiterate what some of today's most respected pretrib scholars have said about Revelation 3:10. Again notice:

- "It's the best exegetical proof of a pretribulational rapture of the Church."
- "It's the determining passage."
- "The Philadelphian church is promised escape from the Tribulation."
- "If there is a "proof text" for the pretribulational position, it is Rev. 3:10."

---

[26] Svigel, "The Apocalypse of John and the Rapture of the Church: a Reevaluation," 28.

- "Rev. 3:10 has remained the primary defense of the position."
- "Here, then, is a promise which clearly indicates the pretribulational rapture of the Church."
- "This promise, however, is to the church of Philadelphia: she will be raptured before the Tribulation begins. It seems difficult to understand why some false teachers suggest that the Church must go through the Tribulation in view of this clear-cut statement of our Lord."
- "One of the best promises guaranteeing the church's rapture before the Tribulation is found in Revelation 3:10."
- "It's the only passage in Revelation to speak of the rapture."
- "This verse promises that the Church will be delivered from the Tribulation."
- "It has the primary understanding of the pretribulational rapture of the Church."
- "We clearly see in this promise that the Church will not go through the Tribulation."
- "There are certain passages of Scripture which definitely promise the Church a removal before the 70th Week."

Based on these statements, whether the pretribulational rapture position stands or falls depends of the interpretation of one verse: Revelation 3:10. If

A Revelation Bombshell

Revelation 3:10 is not a rapture verse, then the pretribulational position does not have any explicit basis in Scripture at all. Only Revelation 3:10 has the claim of being a proof text. So this is a profound and critically important issue.

A Disagreement in the House

In a groundbreaking study published in 2000, Dr. John Niemelä, professor of Hebrew and Greek at Chafer Theological Seminary and another prominent alumnus of the Dallas Theological Seminary, takes exception with the long history of interpretation offered by his fellow pretribulationists. He writes,

> I no longer believe that Revelation 3:10 is a Rapture passage, but it still has relevance to the Rapture. That is, the subject of the verse is not the Rapture, but a larger topic (one that includes the Rapture).[1]

---

[1] John Niemelä, "For You Have Kept My Word: The Theology of Revelation 3:10 (Part 2 of 2)," *CTSJ* 6 (October 2000), 58.

A Revelation Bombshell

Who is this man and what is the basis of his claim? John Niemelä earned Th.M. and Ph.D. degrees in New Testament Literature and Exegesis from Dallas Theological Seminary. Consider the implications. John Niemelä is not anti-pretribulation. He is not antagonistic in any shape, form, or fashion towards the pretrib position. In fact, he remains a devoted and committed supporter of this position. He was part of the pastoral staff at Victor Street Bible Chapel in Dallas, Texas, for seven years. After returning to California (the home of his birth), he taught exegesis at Chafer Theological Seminary for eleven years. He currently ministers as a teaching elder at Grace Chapel of Orange County (California) and serves as researcher for Message of Life Ministries.

Dallas Theological Seminary, Victor Street Bible Chapel, and Grace Chapel of Orange County are all strong advocates of the pretrib rapture. Therefore, we may conclude that Dr. Niemelä is a full-throated and committed proponent of the pretribulation rapture view. In other writings, he has argued strenuously for that position. Thus his denial of Revelation 3:10 as a rapture passage can be accepted without prejudice.

How Dr. Niemelä argues against this long-held position is very interesting. We'll look at this argument and its powerful implications in a minute.

An Exposition of Revelation 3:10: A Proper Translation

Our attempt to gain a correct interpretation of Revelation 3:10 begins with understanding the issues in translation. A comparison of the most popular translations of the New Testament would make it seem that there are no translational difficulties with respect to Revelation 3:10:

KJV   "Because thou hast kept the word of my patience, I also will keep thee from the hour of temptation, which shall come upon all the world, to try them that dwell upon the earth."

NASB   "Because you have kept the word of My perseverance, I also will keep you from the hour of testing, that hour which is about to come upon the whole world, to test those who dwell upon the earth."

NKJV   "Because you have kept My command to persevere, I also will keep you from the hour of trial which shall come upon the whole world, to test those who dwell on the earth."

ESV   "Because you have kept my word about patient endurance, I will keep you from the hour of trial that is coming on the whole world, to try those who dwell on the earth."

A Revelation Bombshell

> **NIV** "Since you have kept my command to endure patiently, I will also keep you from the hour of trial that is going to come upon the whole world to test those who live on the earth."

> **Net Bible** "Because you have kept my admonition to endure steadfastly, I will also keep you from the hour of testing that is about to come on the whole world to test those who live on the earth."

Given the consistency of the English translations, one would think that the grammatical structure of the Greek text that lies behind those translations poses no interpretive challenges. This is not the case. Remember, there is no punctuation in the original manuscripts. The decision to punctuate the text to make the clause "because you have kept my admonition to endure steadfastly" the beginning of verse ten (rather than the end of verse nine) influences the theological conclusion one draws.

Terms like *since* (NIV) and *because* (Net Bible, NASB, ESV, KJV, and NKJV) reflect correctly the translators' decision that the clause *because you have kept my admonition to endure steadfastly* states the cause for an action God takes. But what action is that? In this case, the six translations given above reflect their translators' belief that "because you have kept my admonition to endure steadfastly" is the cause of God's promise to the Philadelphians to "keep you from the hour of testing." While this is a possibility, it is not the only one.

28

In the original Greek text, there are no periods, commas, question marks, or other punctuation. Punctuation is a decision a translator makes based on his or her understanding of the manuscripts. It is just as possible that "because you have kept my admonition to endure steadfastly" is the cause of God's promise in verse nine that he "will make them [the lying false Jews] come and bow down at [the church of Philadelphia's] feet and acknowledge that I have loved you."

Taking this position would result in changing Revelation 3:9-10, which the Net Bible renders as follows:

"Listen! I am going to make those people from the synagogue of Satan—who say they are Jews yet are not, but are lying—Look, I will make them come and bow down at your feet and acknowledge that I have loved you. Because you have kept my admonition to endure steadfastly, I will also keep you from the hour of testing that is about to come on the whole world to test those who live on the earth."

. . . to the following:

"Listen! I am going to make those people from the synagogue of Satan—who say they are Jews yet are not, but are lying—Look, I will make them come and bow down at your feet and acknowledge that I have loved you, because you have kept my admonition to endure steadfastly."

A Revelation Bombshell

Making this change in punctuation, verse 10 would then begin like this:

"Also, I will keep you from the hour of testing that is about to come on the whole world to test those who live on the earth." (Net Bible, with changed punctuation)

This change has profound theological significance on the text. *Enduring steadfastly* is no longer the cause of God's promise to keep the Philadelphians from the hour of testing. There is a profound theological significance to this change. However, before we discuss it, we must prove that this change is grammatically necessary, defensible, and correct.

Why a Change in Punctuation?

To a great degree, we were influenced in our view on this change by a series of articles published by Dr. John Niemelä while a professor of Hebrew and Greek at Chafer Theological Seminary. In one of those articles, published in the *Chafer Theological Seminary Journal* in January 2000, Dr. Niemelä argues with great precision and accuracy that "careful scrutiny reveals a subtle, yet a significant error in most English translations: Revelation 3:10a's causal clause is not subordinate to verse 3:10b, but rather to verse 3:9."[2] Simply stated, the clause "because you have kept my word of patient endurance" goes with verse 9 and not verse 10.

In laymen's terms, this change in punctuation is a more accurate reflection of the normal, natural, and customary relationship between main clause and the subordinate clause in the Greek language. Dr. Niemelä builds his case upon three grammatical and stylistic issues reflected in the Greek text.[3] Dr. Niemelä's proofs are a bit technical for the average layperson, so we shall attempt to paraphrase his conclusions.[4]

First, if adopted, the structure suggested above would make verse 10 begin with the word "also." This reflects the Greek word *kagō* ("and I"), which is a combination of two Greek words: *kai* and *egō*. *Kai* ("and")

> most often serves as a conj[unction]— corresponding to *and*–to link similar parts of sentences or clauses,"[5] i.e. parts of speech that are

---

[2] John Niemelä, "For You Have Kept My Word: The Grammar of Revelation 3:10," *Chafer Theological Seminary Journal* 6 (January 2000), 15.

[3] Ibid., 24.

[4] There is no substitute for reading and understanding Dr. Niemelä's original work in this area. Our apologies to Dr. Niemelä, if, in our attempt to simplify his work, we do not fully convey his intended meaning.

[5] Balz, H. R., and Schneider, G. (1990-). Vol. 2: *Exegetical Dictionary of the New Testament* (227). Grand Rapids, Mich.: Eerdmans.

equal—two sentences, two clauses, two nouns, two verbs. It occurs more than 9,100 times in the New Testament. It is highly unusual for *kai* to connect two parts of speech that are not equal, which is what is required if the traditional punctuation is accepted. In Revelation 3:10, the traditional punctuation attempts to connect an independent clause with a dependent clause.[6]

That is the proverbial mixing of apples and oranges. This conclusion should only be accepted as what John intended if no other conclusion makes sense.

The second word that is a part of the Greek compound term that begins verse 10 is *egō*, which is the first personal pronoun "I," and when used in reference to the speaker serves as an added feature of emphasis. In most cases, *kagō* is to be rendered "I too," especially in taking up a preceding "I" (e.g., Matthew 2:8; 10:32 ff.; Luke 1:3; John 1:31, 33; Acts 8:19; Revelation 3:10).[7] Correctly understood, *kagō* in Revelation 3:10 indicates a third promise.

Therefore, God promises the Philadelphians three things:

---

[6] Dr. Niemelä indicates that only one example of such usage appears in the whole New Testament: 2 Corinthians 11:18.

[7] Balz, H. R., and Schneider, G. (1990-). *Vol. 2: Exegetical Dictionary of the New Testament* (217). Grand Rapids, Mich.: Eerdmans.

1. "I have put in front of you an open door that no one can shut."

2. "I am going to make those people from the synagogue of Satan come and bow down at your feet and acknowledge that I have loved you."

3. "I will keep you from the hour of testing that is about to come on the whole world to test those who live on the earth."

It is important to see that this conclusion better fits the context. Verse 10 states the third of three promises God makes to the Philadelphians. The equality of the promises is maintained when we recognize the correct function of *kagō* at the beginning of verse 10. The traditional interpretation of Revelation 3:10 demands that the basis of the church's removal is faithfulness. That is, the Philadelphian church was so faithful that God promised to remove them. Therefore, each subsequent generation would have to be as faithful as the Philadelphian church in order to claim this promise. Even a casual survey will reveal that this has not been the case down through church history. We as believers have done nothing to warrant removal from the time of testing. This significant detail greatly influences our understanding of this text.

The second support for a change in punctuation concerns the tense of the verbs in Revelation 3:9-10. Each of the verbs (I [Jesus] *will make*; I [Jesus] *will make*; and I [Jesus] *will keep*) is future in focus. Jesus is the subject of each verb. Replacing the comma with a period after "endure steadfastly" ensures that the reader understands the proper relationship between the three. The coordinating conjunction maintains the relationship between them.

The last issue concerns the verb *to keep*. This verb is used three times in Revelation 3:8-10. In the first two instances, it refers to the obedience of the Philadelphians. The last occurrence concerns the deliverance promised by Christ. Replacing (1) the period at the end of Revelation 3:9 with a comma and (2) replacing the comma in Revelation 3:10 with a period clearly distinguishes the relationship between the first two occurrences from the last.

In our view, this is completely necessary. Our faithfulness or lack thereof is not the reason God promises to keep all believers out of the time of testing. One does not have to work hard to realize that not all believers are faithful and deserve to be spared the hour of testing based on their own efforts.

When take all of this together, we are in complete agreement concerning the grammatical correctness of Dr. Niemelä's conclusions.

Following Dr. Niemelä's suggestion, therefore, the NASB would read:

"Behold, I will cause those of the synagogue of Satan, who say that they are Jews, and are not, but lie—behold, I will make them to come and bow down at your feet, and to know that I have loved you, because you have kept the word of My perseverance. And I will keep you from the hour of testing, that hour which is about to come upon the whole world, to test those who dwell upon the earth."

In our estimation, Dr. Niemelä is correct about the punctuation of Revelation 3:10. He is also correct that Revelation 3:10 is not a pretribulation rapture passage. However, we believe he is wrong about the significance of Revelation 3:10 for the rapture question. It does not support a pretrib rapture.

Is Revelation 3:10 a Proof Text?

Is Revelation 3:10 a proof text for a pretribulation rapture? No! Is Revelation 3:10 a proof text for any rapture position? Yes, the prewrath rapture position. The verse does promise that a group of believers will be kept, but not from the seven-year "tribulation period" as the pretribulation rapture view holds. Rather they will be kept from (out) "the hour of testing that is about to come on the whole world to test those who live on the earth."

'Those Who Dwell Upon the Earth'

If the hour of testing is not the seven-year "tribulation period," what is it? What is this "hour" that believers are being kept from? The key to answering this question is the phrase found in the second half of Revelation 3:10: "those who live on the earth."

Those Who Dwell Upon the Earth

God promises to keep believers from "the hour of trial" (or testing) that will come upon the earth "to test those who live [or dwell] the earth." This is a critically important phrase to help us identify the intent of this verse. How does it help? As first noted by Schuler Brown,[1]

---

[1] Schuyler Brown, "The Hour of Trial: Rev. 3:10," *JBL* 85 (Spring 1966), 309.

this exact phrase "those who live [or dwell] on the earth" (depending on your translation) occurs seven times in Revelation. This is extremely relevant because

> [i]n every single case, "those who dwell on the earth" refers to the enemies of God and His people, i.e., to unbelievers. In [Revelation] 6:10 "the inhabitants of the earth" are the persecutors against whom the martyrs cry out for vengeance. In [Revelation] 8:13 the eagle proclaims against them a triple "Woe" because of the three final trumpet calls which are still to come. In [Revelation] 11:10 "the inhabitants of the earth" gloat over the martyrdom of the two witnesses. In [Revelation] 13:8 they worship the beast from the sea; in [Revelation] 13:14 they are deceived by the beast from the land into making an image of the first beast...In [Revelation] 17:8 they gaze in wonder at the scarlet beast...In [Revelation] 13:8 and 17:8 the phrase is further clarified by the clause "whose name is not written in the book of life."[2]

If this phrase does not refer to unbelievers only, it would be the lone exception in the book of Revelation. There is, however, sufficient evidence that it does.

---

[2] Ibid. Brown also indicates that "Where the author requires a phrase with the same conceptual content but without the pejorative moral overtones, he changes the verb . . . [Revelation 14:6]."

A Revelation Bombshell

R. H. Charles correctly identifies the Old Testament definition of the group intended by the equivalent phrase "the inhabitants of the earth." He indicates that both the inhabitants of Palestine and the earth are intended.[3]

Two prophetically significant passages in the Old Testament have direct bearing on this interpretation. Joel 2:1 states, "Blow a trumpet in Zion, and sound an alarm on My holy mountain! Let all *the inhabitants of the land* tremble, for the day of the Lord is coming; surely it is near" (italics added). In this passage, Joel speaks of the impact of the day of the Lord for Judah. At the time of the eschatological fulfillment of this prophecy, Judah will exist in unbelief.

Zephaniah 1:18 broadens the phrase to include the whole world. Notice,

> "Neither their silver nor their gold will be able to deliver them on the day of the Lord's wrath; and all the earth will be devoured in the fire of His jealousy, for He will make a complete end, indeed a terrifying one, of all *the inhabitants of the earth*." (emphasis added)

In light of Zephaniah 1:18, Isaiah 26:20-21 is very significant. Isaiah writes,

---

[3] R. H. Charles, *The International Critical Commentary* (Edinburgh: T&T Clark, 1994), 289.

"Come, my people, enter into your rooms, and close your doors behind you; hide for a little while until indignation runs its course. For behold, the Lord is about to come out from His place to punish *the inhabitants of the earth* for their iniquity; and the earth will reveal her bloodshed, and will no longer cover her slain." (emphasis added)

Isaiah indicates that God will "punish the inhabitants of the earth" because of their iniquity. Carl Schultz, writing in the *Theological Wordbook of the Old Testament*, explains that in the Hebrew, the term "iniquity" is a collective noun. "In instances too numerous to list, this term is a collective, or a quasi-abstract, noun denoting the sum of past misdeeds against God and man."[4]

Particular attention should be given to the context of Isaiah 26:21. Notice, "the earth will also disclose her blood, and will no more cover her slain." The latter portion of the verse highlights the particular group of individuals foremost in the mind of God when his day-of-the-Lord wrath is poured out against all unbelievers.

Delitzsch indicates that the earth supplies two witnesses to this fact:

---

[4] Carl Schultz, s.v. *awoni*, *Theological Wordbook of the Old Testament*, 2:651.

A Revelation Bombshell

> (1) the innocent blood which has been violently shed...which is now exposed, and cries for vengeance; and (2) the persons themselves who have been murdered in their innocence, and who are slumbering within her. Streams of blood come to light and bear testimony, and martyrs arise to bear witness against their murderers.[5]

In essence, then, Isaiah 26:21 answers the question of the fifth seal martyrs of Revelation 6:10: "When are you going to avenge our blood on those who dwell on the earth?" The answer is that God will avenge their blood during his day-of-the-Lord wrath. Therefore, we conclude that unbelievers are the group upon whom the hour of testing or temptation will fall.

Four Reasons "the Hour of Trial" Is the Day of the Lord Wrath

Can we be sure that the "hour of trial [or testing]" is God's day of the Lord wrath and not the great

---

[5] Franz Delitzsch, *Biblical Commentary on the Prophecies of Isaiah*, Vol. 1 (Grand Rapids: Eerdmans Publishing Company, 1969), 453.

tribulation? Yes. Let's look at four reasons why this is the case.

Reason #1: The Nature of the Testing

The first reason is the nature of the testing. God tests and Satan tempts. The word *periazo* (to test or tempt) doesn't distinguish between the two. In itself, *peirazo* can be used either way.[6]

God tests men in the positive sense. He tests them to discover their nature or character. God tested Abraham in order to discover whether he feared God (Gen. 22:12). God tested the children of Israel to discover whether they would obey him (Judges 2:22). Jesus tested Philip to determine whether he knew of a solution to feed the five thousand. Peter indicates that both the destruction with

---

[6] BADG indicates that *Peirazw* has two basic meanings: to try or attempt in the sense to try and fail, and (2) to try, make trial of, or put to the test to discover what kind of a person someone is. In this second category, there is a good and bad sense. In a bad sense, a person is tested in order to discover something about his or her nature or character in order to use it against them or to tempt them to cause them to sin. In a positive sense, one tests someone to discover positive qualities in his or her nature or character. James 1:13 indicates that God never tempts a person in the sense of causing someone to sin; neither does God need to test a person to find a reason to condemn. However, God does test men in order to discover their nature or character. Abraham (Gen. 22:1, Heb. 11:17), Philip (John 6:6), and the children of Israel (Ex. 20:20, Ju. 2:22) were all tested by God in this sense.

respect to the flood and that of Sodom and Gomorrah were tests of God against the ungodly.[7]

Satan, on the other hand, *tempts*. Scripture speaks specially of a worldwide deception that Satan sponsors. In fact, it speaks of two of them. One occurs before Armageddon (Rev. 16:13-16) and one occurs after it (Rev. 20:7-10).

In the hour of trial, is God testing the hearts of unbelievers or is Satan tempting or deceiving them?

This particular trial or temptation referred to in Revelation 3:10 covers the "whole world." But this doesn't really help us since both God and Satan "tempt" on a worldwide basis.

Jesus indicated that the day of the Lord would affect the whole world (Matt. 24:30; Luke 21:35). Peter also indicates that the day of the Lord would be worldwide in nature (2 Pet. 3:10). The Old Testament prophets indicated this, as well (Is. 13:11, 13; Zeph. 3:8). However, God's wrath centers on unbelievers.

The deception of Satan/Antichrist, on the other hand, is worldwide but his wrath directed toward Israel (the woman, Rev. 12:13) and believers ("her [Israel's] offspring, who keep the commandments of God and have the testimony of Jesus," Rev. 12:17). Thus the persecution under

---

[7] See 2 Peter 2:9.

Satan/Antichrist will be worldwide geographically, but only those who refuse to worship him will experience this wrath. Those who willingly submit will not face persecution, but Satan/Antichrist's supposed protection.

Therefore, "the hour of testing" cannot be the persecution under Satan/Antichrist since the hour of trial is directed, not toward Israel and believers (as Satan/Antichrist's wrath is), but toward "those who dwell on the earth." Therefore, while this testing (or trial) will be worldwide, we believe *the hour of trial* refers to the day of the Lord because the purpose[8] of the trial is "to test those who dwell on the earth."

Reason #2: The Church Is Not Promised Wholesale Deliverance

The second reason the phrase "the hour of trial" refers to the day of the Lord is that the church is not promised wholesale deliverance from the great tribulation, which is better termed the persecution under Satan/Antichrist.

The Lord promised the church of Philadelphia, "I will keep you away from hour of trial." Clearly, the church is not promised to be kept out from the midst of the persecution of the Antichrist (Rev. 12:17; 13:7; 2 Thess. 2:3; Matt. 24:22) because many believers will die

---

[8] *Peirazw* is used as an infinitive of purpose here.

during this time (Matt. 24:9). In fact, Matthew 24:29 indicates that God evacuates his elect immediately after the tribulation under Satan/the Antichrist is cut short.

The discourse in Luke 21, which parallels the Olivet Discourse of Matthew/Mark in many places (and yet differs in a substantial way), offers support for this conclusion. Luke records the Lord's sermon concerning the A.D. 70 destruction of Jerusalem and the persecution that Israel will experience in connection with it. Luke 21:12-19 specifically addresses the persecution the disciples themselves will experience in connection with this destruction. Luke 21:20-24 is the most complex portion of Luke's discourse. In a beautiful example of a near/far prophecy, Luke foretells both the A.D. 70 destruction of Jerusalem (the near) and the final destruction of Jerusalem (the far) during the Seventieth Week of Daniel at the hands of the Antichrist and his armies.[9]

Van Kampen writes, "The Jerusalem Campaign which will occur at the midpoint of the seventieth week—at which time Antichrist will move his armies against Jerusalem, set up his throne in the Temple, and demand the world's worship,"[10] will immediately be followed by the great tribulation.

---

[9] Robert Van Kampen in *The Sign* correctly identified and labeled the far event as "The Jerusalem Campaign."
[10] Robert Van Kampen, *The Sign* (Wheaton: Crossway Books, 1993), 275.

However, one should quickly notice that while Luke describes the A.D. 70 destruction of the temple, in verses 25-28, he moves to the events connected with the day of the Lord. Luke records the earthly and heavenly phenomena that are consistently portrayed as the signs that signal the imminent arrival of this eschatological day. The sign in the sun, moon, and stars with disturbances on earth is detailed in Joel 2:28-32 and 3:15-16; Isaiah 13:10, 34:4; and Haggai 2:6. That Luke 21:25-28 concerns the *parousia* of Christ, which involves both the rapture of the church and the wrath of God against the wicked that remain, is borne out by verse 28. It states, "But when these things [the earthly and heavenly disturbances][11] begin to take place, straighten up and lift up your heads, because your redemption is drawing near."

Reason #3: The Use of Luke's Figures of Speech

The third reason the "hour of trial" refers to the day of the Lord, not the great tribulation, comes from these two very important figures of speech used by Luke: "straighten up" and "lift up your heads."[12]

---

[11] In contradistinction to Darrell L. Bock, *Luke 9:51- 24:53* (Grand Rapids: Baker Books, 1996, 1686, footnote 41), who includes the appearing of Jesus Christ as one of "these things."

[12] Bullinger identifies the particular figure of speech used here as a metonymy of the adjunct, which he defines as "some circumstance pertaining to the subject is put for the subject itself." In this particular

A Revelation Bombshell

"Lift up your heads" as a figure of speech occurs only once in the New Testament, but it appears in three different passages in the Old Testament. A look at these three passages will help clarify Luke's intent.

Judges 8:28 indicates that "Midian was subdued before the sons of Israel," with the result that "they [the Midianites] did not lift up their heads anymore." The Hebrew verb translated *subdued* "denotes bringing a proud and recalcitrant people or spirit into subjection."[13]

Psalm 82:3 also uses this key phrase. The Psalmist laments that his enemies have "exalted themselves," which in the Hebrew literally says, "they have lifted the head." The Psalmist, in turn, asks God to "deal with them as with Midian" (Psalm 83:9). In other words, humble them so that "they do not lift up their heads anymore."

The third passage that contains this key phrase is Zechariah 1:21. Judah, Israel, and Jerusalem have been scattered by the Gentile nations with the result "that no man lifts up his head." As with the previous references, military subjection has resulted in a people's inability "to lift up their heads."

That pride and humility are connected with the notion of a head lifted up can be clearly seen from Job

---

case, the sign is put for the thing signified. The "lifting of the head" signifies joy or courage.

[13] *Theological Wordbook of the Old Testament*, s.v. *kana.'*

10:15-16. Notice, "If I am wicked, woe to me! and if I am righteous, I dare not lift up my head. I am sated with disgrace and conscious of my misery. And should my head be lifted up, thou wouldst hunt me like a lion." In 9:1-10:22, Job responds to the speech of Bildad, who explains Job's sufferings as the result of some sin in Job's life. Bildad bases his position on the teachings of the fathers (Job 8:8-10). Job refutes these claims with the fact since God created him, he knows his heart. Since God knows his heart, he keeps an account of his sin and demands just recompense (Job 10:14). Given that this is the way God works, Job says, "If I am guilty—woe to me! Even if I am innocent, I cannot lift my head, for I am full of shame and drowned in my affliction" (Job 10:15, NIV). The New International Version does a nice job of translating this verse. Job's point is clear: to be suffering as he is, even if he is innocent, does not allow him "to raise his head cheerfully."[14]

The use of this figure of speech in the Old Testament informs Luke's meaning in 21:28. Prior to the Lord's return to evacuate the church, believers will exist in a state of shame or affliction.

Paul writes in 2 Thessalonians 1:6-7,

---

[14] Franz Delitzsch, *Biblical Commentary on The Book of Job*, Vol. 1 (Grand Rapids: Eerdmans Publishing Company, 1968), 169.

A Revelation Bombshell

> For after all it is only just for God to repay with affliction *those who afflict you* and to give relief to *you who are afflicted* and to us as well when the Lord Jesus shall be revealed from heaven with His mighty angels in flaming fire dealing out retribution to those who do not know God and those who do not obey the gospel of our Lord Jesus. (emphasis added)

Paul uses the same Greek term to describe the situation of the Thessalonians as was used in the Old Testament (LXX) to describe the afflictions of both Job and Israel. Matthew 24:21 indicates that a "great tribulation" will take place during the time immediately before the return of Christ. Matthew uses the same term as does Paul—the same term that is used in the OT (LXX) that causes the people to have heads hung down. The affliction of God's elect will be alleviated just after the sign is given in the sun, moon, and stars, but prior to the actual wrath of God's day of the Lord.

Luke uses a second, complementary phrase in Luke 21:28: "straighten up," which confirms our understanding. The Greek word Luke uses here literally means "to straighten up from a bent over position and focuses on the reversal of a process."[15]

---

[15] Louw and Nida, s.v. *anakuptw*

What event will have God's people in a figurative sense "bent over?" It can be none other than the persecution under Satan/Antichrist, which the Lord will "cut short" with his appearing at the start of the day of the Lord.

Reason #4: The Use of the Article "The"

The fourth and final reason "the hour of testing" refers to the day of the Lord is Jesus' use of tiny, seemingly insignificant three-letter word: *the*.

The day of the Lord is the most well-known eschatological event prophesied in the Bible. Unlike the great tribulation, which appears in Daniel (9:27, 12:1), Matthew (24:15), and Revelation, the day of the Lord occurs in both the Major and Minor Prophets. It also occurs in the writings of Paul, Peter, James, and John.

This bears heavily on our discussion because Revelation 3:10 says *the* hour of testing. In the Greek, the article *the* has several functions. Here, the article of par excellence fits best. Daniel Wallace indicates that the article of par excellence "is frequently used to point out a substantive that is, in a sense, 'in a class by itself.' It is the only one deserving of the name . . . . The par excellent article is not necessarily used just for the best of a class. It

A Revelation Bombshell

could be used for the worst of a class . . . . In essence, par excellence indicates the extreme of a particular class."[16]

This hour of testing is the worst hour the unbelievers will ever know because it is the day of the Lord's wrath.

Defining 'the Hour of Testing'

The Lord promised the Philadelphians that they would be kept from "the hour of testing." What future event is described this way? Many simply indicate that it refers to the great tribulation. Unfortunately, due to their incorrect assumptions about the purpose of Revelation 3:10, pretribulationists had to force several conclusions on this verse to make it fit their theological system. Robert L. Thomas' words are typical when he writes, "[The i]dentification of...'the hour of trial' is not difficult....It is to be a time of distress on the world before the coming of Christ, one known as the day of the Lord, the Tribulation, or the Great Tribulation."[17]

As we have seen in these pages, this is a mistake. This conclusion fails to distinguish between the great

---

[16] Wallace, *Greek Grammar Beyond the Basics*, 222.
[17] Robert L. Thomas, *Revelation 1-7: An Exegetical Commentary* (Chicago: Moody Press, 1992), 288-289. Robert H. Mounce, *The Book of Revelation* (Grand Rapids: Eerdmans Publishing Co., 1977), 119. John F. Walvoord, *The Revelation of Jesus Christ* (Chicago: Moody Press, 1989), 87.

tribulation, which is the wrath of Satan against God's elect, and the day of the Lord, which is the wrath of God against the wicked. This has also led pretribulationists to incorrectly identify the precise meaning of the phase *the hour of trial.*

The "hour of trial" does not refer to the persecution by Satan and his Antichrist during Daniel's Seventieth Week. It refers to the day of the Lord.[18]

The conclusion? Revelation 3:10 is not a promise of deliverance from the persecution under Satan/Antichrist. Rather, it is *a promise of escape from the day of the Lord's wrath.*

---

[18] Dr. Allen R. Kerkeslager correctly identifies "the hour of testing" as the day of the Lord. However, he limits this "day" to a literal 24-hour day and "the hour of testing" to the literal hour of the Lord's *parousia*. See his unpublished paper presented at the Annual Meeting of the Society of Biblical Literature in Kansas City, Missouri, November 23-26, 1991.

What About 'the Hour'?

What about the term "the hour"? How does this impact the discussion?

The Lord's promise to keep the Philadelphians from or out of "the hour of testing" is unique in terms of the way the promise is worded. *The hour* is not an uncommon phrase in John's literature. It occurs over thirty times. It can refer to a specific hour of the day (e.g., 12 noon) or "the time set for something,"[1] without reference to a specific hour of the day. It is the second sense that is of interest to us at this point. The use of *hour* to designate a period of time has biblical support.

---

[1] Gerhard Delling, *The Theological Dictionary of the New Testament*, Vol. IX (Grand Rapids: Eerdmans Publishing Co., 1959), 677.

Lenski writes, "John repeatedly mentioned this 'hour'...it is not a part of a day but a special period of time."[2]

In a majority of cases, the specific hour is not defined. However, "the hour" in Revelation 3:10b has a genitive phrase following it that clearly defines the intent as being more than a sixty-minute period.

We list several other occurrences of this phenomenon in the New Testament:

Luke 1:10	the hour of the incense offering
Luke 14:17	the hour of the banquet
Luke 22:53	the hour of them (chief priests, officers of the temple and elders)
John 16:21	the hour of her (to give birth)
Acts 3:1	the hour of prayer
Rev. 14:7	the hour of his judgment
Rev. 14:15	the hour to reap[3]

In the case of Revelation 3:10, the specific time period of "the hour" is defined by the genitive phrase "of trial/testing" (*peirasmou*).

---

[2] R. H. C. Lenski, *The Interpretation of St. John's Gospel* (Minneapolis: Augsburg Publishing House, 1961), 904.

[3] Revelation 14:15 does not include a genitive, but an infinitive of purpose.

A Revelation Bombshell

As we have discussed, *peirasmos* has two nuances. Louw and Nida suggest one is "to try to learn the nature or character of someone or something by submitting such to thorough and extensive testing—'to test, to examine, to put to the test, examination, testing.'"[4] A second nuance is "to endeavor or attempt to cause someone to sin—'to tempt, to trap, to lead into temptation, temptation.'"[5] Context determines which nuance the author intends.

In this context, we believe the author intends the first because while the Philadelphians are delivered, the earth-dwellers are not. Since God never "tempts" man to sin and the earth-dwellers are known by their evil deeds, it is clearly the intent of the text to emphasize a test to expose the heart condition of those tested. In this case, the earth-dwellers are put to the test. God is the tester and the earth-dwellers are the tested.

---

[4] Louw and Nida, s.v. *peirasmos* (§27.46).
[5] Ibid.

What Does It Mean for You?

There are two events depicted in the Bible that are stated to be unparalleled in nature: the eschatological day of the Lord and the eschatological wrath of Satan/Antichrist.

The physical expression of God's wrath during the future day of the Lord will be the worst wrath of God unbelievers will ever know. Joel 2:2 states, "There has never been anything like it, nor will there be again after it to the years of many generations." In contradistinction, the wrath of Satan/Antichrist, which believers and some in Israel will experience during the second half of Daniel's Seventieth Week, will be the worst persecution the elect of God will ever experience. Matthew 24:21 states, "For then there will be a great tribulation, such as has not occurred since the beginning of the world until now, nor ever shall [be]."

The great tribulation is the wrath of Satan through his instrument, the Antichrist (Rev. 12:12, 13:5). Since *the hour of trial* has as its object "those who dwell upon the earth," which we conclude refers to unbelievers, then it is right to conclude that "the hour of testing" refers to the day of the Lord—God's eschatological wrath and not the seven-year "tribulation period" as pretribulationists believe.

This finding is consistent with all the other promises in the New Testament that God's elect living on the earth just prior to the Lord's return will be evacuated to the clouds and escape the wrath of God. God's eschatological wrath is the only wrath every single believer has ever been promised to the believer but the grace of God through Jesus Christ, our Lord. Amen!

What Do You Think?

So does Revelation 3:10 prove beyond a shadow of a doubt that a pretribulation rapture is the correct view of Scripture? If you believed that before, what do you say now? Are you really willing to put your future in the hands of a system that does not have one explicit verse of support in the whole Bible?

For more information on how to endure the great tribulation that is coming, see these other books by Charles Cooper:

God's Elect and the Great Tribulation: An Interpretation of Matthew 24:1-31 and Daniel 9

Fight, Flight, or Faith: How to Survive the Great Tribulation

A Revelation Bombshell

About the Author

Charles Cooper is a pastor, lecturer, writer, and director of the Prewrath Resource Institute. He is the author of numerous articles, booklets, and *God's Elect and the Great Tribulation: An Exposition of Matthew 24:1–31 and Daniel 9* and *Fight, Flight, or Faith: How to Survive the Great Tribulation*. Cooper is a 1986 graduate of Dallas Theological Seminary.

www.ingramcontent.com/pod-product-compliance
Lightning Source LLC
Chambersburg PA
CBHW071024040426
42443CB00007B/916